T0193885

GIVE BACK
— TO YOUR —
ETHNIC
COMMUNITY

Donald Sharief

authorHOUSE®

AuthorHouse™
1663 Liberty Drive
Bloomington, IN 47403
www.authorhouse.com
Phone: 1 (800) 839-8640

Published by AuthorHouse 10/15/2019

ISBN: 978-1-7283-3179-9 (sc)
ISBN: 978-1-7283-3180-5 (e)

Print information available on the last page.

We African American have the resources to have our own community. All we have to do is give back together. Back in the thirties, we were very poor, and we did not have the money to build our own community. We have come a long way from slavery. When we did not have money, we had more unity! Sometimes when people don't have money, they show more unity. When the Temptations first started out with Motown, they made an oath that they would always be together. Otis, one of them, said, "What happens when the money starts getting good?" And attitude started to happen in the group. That's what happens to African Americans. Having money should not change us; it should make us more giving. Rappers like 50 Cent should be giving back because he doesn't want to see anyone coming up the way he did. Some African Americans are making millions from other African Americans and not giving back to their ethnic community. We should not support them. By not supporting them, we will produce people who do what they do and will love to give back to their ethnic community. When you see all of us, as a whole, being rich, that's success. We don't want to just see Oprah being rich. And we need to preserve our history. I was in Harlem and saw a statue of Harriet Tubman. I asked a young African American woman who worked there, "Who is that statue of?" She did not know. I said to her, "You should be a shamed of yourself. Some of us cannot go past Dr. King or Malcom X. It would be easy to know our history if we had our own— we must not forget people like Imam W. Deen Mohammed, Elijah Mohammed, and Frad Mohammed, and we must not forget about Hank Aaron, who broke Babe Ruth's record in baseball. When you do something big like that, you deserve credit for it. Some of us know about Dr. King and Malcolm because the news media talk of them. When we have our own, we can say what we want. We should produce the things we need. If we produce some of the TV shows, we can say what we want. African American magazines that produce their own content should write more about our history. And basically, that's what this book is all about. The honorable Elijah Mohammed helped *Ebony* magazine avoid going out of business. *Ebony* was not doing well in magazine sales. Back in those days, brothers were selling *Muhammed Speaks* newpapers on the street. Elijah Mohammed had the brothers sell *Ebony* magazine on the streets. He helped churches out too; he was not helping Muslims only. We should not be selfish people. There was an elder man in the neighborhood. He said to me, "Most Negros, when they start living better, think they are better. And Pappy was a man we all respected. Back in the thirties, we were called Negroes. Some people would rather talk about you than help: that must stop. I hear people talking about Nicki Minaj. They say things that are destructive about her. I think all rappers should have a positive character. I feel good seeing someone who looks like me doing well. I hope Nicki keeps doing well. That's how we are supposed to feel about each other. When we have that kind of love for each other, we can live together in peace. If we are going to talk about each other, it should be constructive criticism. Like I said about the rappers, they should have good character. And they should show it in their music. We don't want to come together just when someone dies. I have a niece who lives in Philadelphia; I live in New York. I called my niece one week in advance to tell her that I was coming to

Philadelphia. I was there three days at a hotel, and she did not come to visit me there. When my mother passed, the whole family was there. There is a old saying: black people don't come together until someone dies. Some people, as long as everything is all right in their immediate families or themselves—that's all they are concerned with. When someone says destructive things about you, don't feed into it by responding. The devil wants to see us fighting each other; don't be the aggressor. We don't want our small children using the f-word. Saying all rappers should not use the f-word in their songs is constructive criticism. And rappers should not be dogging each other in their songs. Constructive criticism promotes improvement; that's what we want. And don't go too far with constructive criticism. Sometimes, we have to say nothing. I will not say or do something that will stop a person's success. You would not want anyone to stop you. Tererai Trent was on *The Oprah Winfrey Show*. She is from Zimbabwe. She came to this country, went to school, got her degree, and went back to her country to give back. Oprah said that's what she is saying on her show. That's how you build community. Whatever problems we are having, let's stay together and work through our problems. Trent was living in a hut; she did not have running water. With all this wealth in the world, people should not be in poverty. If there were not enough in creation, you could blame G-d. Humans are at fault because humans are greedy. G-d is perfect; look at his creation. Some people have too much money, just like some people don't have enough. The late Iman W. D. Mohammed was not trying to make a lots of money for himself. He was trying to show us how we all can have it. That's what a good leader does. We have to stop our selfish ways and share. When you make money, put some back, like Magic Johnson. He has opened up movie theaters in the communty. If we don't do it, no one is going to do it for us. I would rather give a million dollars to charity than spend a million dollars on something that I do not need. On the day of judgment, G-d is going judge you on how you spend your wealth. There are people living in poor countries who do not have running water or electricity. There was a hurricane in New York and New Jersey; some of the people don't have running water or electricity because of the hurricane. What if you had to live like that every day, like people do in poor countries? Nobody should have to live like that with all this modern technology in the world. Things happen for a reason. The way people are helping each other because of the hurricane is how we should be helping people in poor countries. The whole world should have the same material things. That's how G-d wants it to be! You should feel good to please G-d. All of us should live our lives in a way that we are ready to give. Back in the sixties, when they first started out with Motown, the singing group the Temptations had more unity. In the beginning, they did not have money. Otis Williams, one of the Temptations, said, "What happened when the money started getting good? People in the group started getting attitude." That's what happened to African Americans as we started making money. Back in the thirties, we had more unity. There was no envy and jealously because we were very poor. We did not have much education. As soon as we started living better, we started having problems like the Temptations. I was in a beauty supply store that sells all African American products. The store is owned by someone who is not African American. If we were giving back like we should, we would be providing the things we need. That's all I am trying to say. The reason I think African Americans do not have their own ethnic community is the ones who have money do not give back, or only a small percentage do. That is not enough! We are not self-sufficient. We have to meet our needs. Charity starts at home and spreads. Look at how African Americans like Frederick Douglass and Harriet Tubman gave back in slavery. After they were free, they started helping other slaves be free. Love for yourself what you love for your brother. They did not feel comfortable having freedom and seeing other slaves still in slavery. You should feel the same way about the community. Don't just get rich and buy a big house in someone else's community. Let's try to solve some of the problems we have in our community. There has to be a reason why so many African Americans are locked up. Having favorable opportunities will make things better. This is how you help people get out of prison. Some of us get rich and forget where we come from. We just think about ourselves and our families. We have to think about each other. When you just think about yourself and your family, you are not helping anyone but yourself and your family. We don't want to separate ourselves from each other; we need to bond. When you forget where you come from, something will happen to bring you down to reality. Nigger, you think you are better than me—that's why you forgot where you came from. When I say "nigger," don't just think black people—there are white niggers too. I have seen how when some African American start living better, they think they are better, even if it's just having a new car. I have had so-called friends like that; I had to stop going around with them. Maybe we should just take the time to thank G-d that we want be like that. Whatever G-d blesses me with, I am thankful! No matter how big or small the blessing is, I am grateful. Being grateful opens up the doors for more blessings. I have had women who were ungrateful bitches! When you are ungrateful, one day the blessings will stop coming. Some people complain all the time and don' t have a good reason to. We want people in our community who will lift us up. We are already being discriminated against. I did not agree with Bill Cosby's comment. He said you, s can not go to college taking like that. We need him to give us courage, that witii make us feel good about ourself. Jf you talk to people in a positive way, that will give them courage. You don, t say negative things to people, that all ready is having a hard time. They need to hear something positive, to motivate them in the right direction. Jf he was not rich, he would not be saying that. J have seen african american on tv talking about there children. Because he is rich with pride, he say my daugther go to duke, and he should be happy. There is know reason why, rich children should not do good, they have favorable opportunity. Jf you want to be proud, go on tv talking about how you have sent african american to college that could not aford to go. That, s better then saying, i have one daugther just finsh college, and a other one just staring. African american as a whole, must have good opportunity to. It should disturb you to see how some of us is living. Jndividually some of us are doing good, as a whole we are not. We want all of us to do good, and we can make it happen. J was watching charlie rose intervien jz the raper, and he ask him with all this money, you are making how are you giving back. He did not give a good answer to the question. J think we should not support them, if they don, t give back to us. Ask the people where you live, to support you. We will produce people that do what you do, and love to give back to there ethnic community, you can be replace. Just think of the african american that are rich, the ones that can aford to give one million dollar. We would be a lots farther a head. We don, t have to do illegal things to get ahead, if we all give back. It have to happen from the top, they have the most money. To much is given much is exspect, and it should be like that. Because there are so many, of us lockup when my daughter, come home with a new man the frist question, i ask have he been to prison. That, s a question that should not have to come up. People with favorable opportunity don, t have that problem. When african american stop going to prison, that mean we are on the street living productive lives. Not on the street doing illegal things. We don, t want to be look down as criminal. We want to be look up, as respectful citizen. There was a big time durg dealar in the neighborhood, my son said to me that he admiral him. J said to him why would you, admiral someone that is doing life in prison. He said i mean, the money he was making. J don, t admiral him for the money, look at what it cost him. We have to get that kind of thinking, out of our mind. We want our youth to grow up being law abiding citizen. Went i was a young boy, a white man ask this young boy, what do you want to do for a living, he said a durg dealar. That, s the kind of mentality, that we need to stop. Having. And the rapper are not helping, because there mentality are the same. Jceberg slim wrote a book in the sixties, about his life as a pimp. Lots of young african american men, read that book wanting to be a pimp. Jceberg slim said they don, t understand the book. That kind of life made a heroin addict out of him, and his life was full of redemption. He said the book is more about redemption. Jn other words he was not trying, to glamourize pimping. He was trying to change, the way he was living. That, s why he said my life was full of redemption, and it made a heroin addict out of him. We have to stop glamourize all kind of street life. J don, t have to tell you where that, kind of life will get us. We are putting the wrong things back, in the community. Our children should grow up wanting to be respectful, not breaking the law. And than we don, t have to worry about them. We have to do positive things, in the community that will want us to change. We have to so round ourself with positive things. Jf we don, t give back we will still have, the same problem. When you don, t give back you are just thinking, about yourself. And in the end you will be the loser. You have to understand, what wealth is for, wealth is for to serve man. Jf man was using his wealth to serve man, you would not have so much poverty in the world. Sometimes having wealth can do more harm, then good to you. Speoucialty went you don, t use your wealth right. Because of your greed someone have to suffer. And that, s when you are not using, your wealth to serve man. There is so much in creation, man cannot use what, s in creation up. So there is know reason why there should be poverty. There are too manny people in the world, that make too much money, the more they get the more they want. And you have to manny people in the world that don, t make enough money. Everbody should make enough money to live, above the poverty line. And it is government duty to make it happen. And they make too much, money to not be doing a good job. Jf the politician were doing a good job, people would not be struggle to live. It should be in the constitution, that all american live in a adequate housing. You should not have to work, two jobs to pay your rent. The mayor in new york city live rent free, why should you have to struggle to pay your rent, we need fordable housing. And we would not have a homeless problem. And you would not have to struggle, to pay your rent. As much as money the mayor make he don, t need free rent. The people that need help, don, t get that kind of help that is not fare. A person that is struggleing to pay his rent, or a person that is homeless do he feel proud to be american?i can see why politician are proud to be american, look at what the country is doing for them. Look how good they are living, and the money they are making. Politician give back by helping people to live better. Are the american people, happy with the job they are doing?there are too many people struggle to live, in this country. J don, t have to spell everthing out to you, you see how the american people are living. J am not happy with the job they are doing, rather they are democracy or republican. Why because people should not have to struggle, to pay for necessity things, politician should make it happen. For years people have been struggleing, to pay for necessity things. You should not have to go hungry in this country, food is a necessity. You should not even have to go to food banks, there is too much money. The money is going some where, but not in the right places. Jf the money was going in the right places, people would not be suffering. We need better politicians, so the job will be done right. This country have to much to offer, that, s why everbody want to come here, everbody want to live better. You cannot blame them. People in poor countrys don, t have running water, or electricity. But the politicians are living good. People in poor countrys should not, have to go hungry. The government can at lease, make sure everbody have a hot meal everday, and that is a necessity. The government cocern should be the welfare, of the people. The people have to stop suffering, while government live good, it have to be a balance. That is not to say there is a balance in this country, no it is not. You help those more who need help, the most.

The rich don, t need help, they should be giving back more. When i say give back to your ethnic community, i am talking about the whole world, we are all children of adam. We are one human family, we need to show it more. If we treat each other, like we have the same father and mother, it would be better. Because we would show more love, for each other. And we would give more to each other. Some of us just think of, ourself and family, there is a world of people. And there is so much to give, to the world. Giving will change the conditions in the world, and make you a better preson. To a lots of people it, s all about money!we should never put money above, the welfare of people. We may want to be rich, but if you use your wealth in the wrong way, it can do you more harm then good. Having wealth should have you giving more money. Jf you do it that way, you are using your weath the right way. We have to understand what is wealth for, wealth is for to serve man with. Some people make millions and go broke. Maybe if they were using there weal right, they would not have went broke. You will have a better change keeping your wealth, using it right. Some people are spend thrift, someone who waste fullessly spend money. Went they can be giving back what they waste. No matter how much money you make, you should never waste. J see some african american go out and buy big price idume, that they don, t need and go broke. What do you exspect, when you spend money like that. J try to spend money like it, s my last, and yet it, s not. The raper little wayne was sued for two millions dollars, by a company that lease jets, he did not win the case. It would have made more sense giving two millions dollars, back to his ethnic community. Then to waste two millions dollars on something, he did not need. Why should african american support him, if he don, t give back to his ethnic community. Where you spend your money, is where you should get your support. There are african american out there, that is just as good as you are or better, that can do what you do, all they need is a break. And they will be happy to give back to there ethnic community, knowing this is why they got a break. There is a reason why people are rich, g-d must have seen fit for you to be rich. Now that you are there don, t miss used it, don, t be a spend thrift. We all like having nice things, don, t go over borer, you have to respect money. There may be a time in life where you don, t have it, like that. There have been a time in my life, where i was dead broke, i did not have coffee money. J was telling that to a friend, i said no i did not have fifty cent, to buy a cup of coffee. She made a joke out of it, she said a cup of coffee cost at lease one dollar now. She did not understand how could i have got that broke, believe me it can happen. To someone who have not experience that, and don, t understand life, cannot see how that can happen. There was a time in my life, where i was thinking the same way. J was young and did not understand life. A person about fourty should know better. Even if it have not happen to you. Because of the years you have been living, and experience life. Don, t think you are so hight and mighty, and you cannot get broke. You can be so broke that you hit rock bottom. When you are homeless and need help, to get back on your feet. You may have to go live in a shelter, times can get that hard. J know because i have experience hard times, like that. You have to get help from some where, to get back on your feet. You have no money, no where to live, no food to eat, you have to seek assistance. J had no momey, i was behine on my rent, had no food to eat. J had to seek assistance. J ask a brother can i borrow some money, he said yes but he don, t have it right now. When he come back he will have it. J waited for him in dunkin donuts, when he did come back he said he did not have it. He ask me to wait again. The next day i saw him, he said you did not wait, i came back. J said to him, i can still used it if you have it. He said i don, t have it, when i come back i will have it. J did not bother him no more. When you ask for a favor, just say yes or no. J think that brother did not have, the money. He felt bad because he did not have it, and did not want to say it. J did not feel back asking. J ask one other brother for a favor, can i receive phone calls from his phone. J was looking for a job, and did not have a phone. That did not work out. J ask a nother borther, can i used his car, to take my road test to get my driverlicense back. He said yes, when it came time he could not do it. J had said to him i need this for a job. J did not get the favors, i still need help. G-d open up a way for me. J got my license back, and the things i need. Do not depend on man. J got welfare, for about theree month. J receive emergency food stemps, and a check. And that was a relief. J was living day by day at that time, and was about to get evicted. We have to understand, what the word brother means. A brother is a helper, and protector. We african american, used that word all the time. J don, t think some of us understand, the meaning of that word. Beause of the way, some of us treat each other. You don, t miss treat your brother. It don, t have to be, mental or physical. Jf your brother need help, and you don, t help him, you are miss treating him or us. Jf you don, t give back to your ethnic community. You are miss treating your brothers and sisters. Why? Because you are rich, we know the ones can make a differren. Don, t take charity as something lite. Charity in all religion is a obligation. G-d made it a obligation!i don, t care how rich or poor someone is, they should not have to live in filthy condition. No matter where they live in the world. We should live like we are human being. And there is no excuse, that you can give to justify it. Cleanliess is next to g-d liness. The frist thing you have to do to worship g-d is be clean. There are some landlords, that do not keep up there building. The city should not let them rent apartment, that are not well keep up. Some people have to be force to do right. You should not have to be force, to make the apartments, clean and safe to live in. It is inhuman to live in filthy condition. All human being should live in clean, fordable housing. We are not animals. Why should we live like animals. Man is king of g-d creation. And we should live like we are kings. It should be a law, that all people live in clean, fordable housing. And that will stop, people living in filthy condition. Human being have rights. You have to respect a person, because he or she is a human being. Jf you let someone, live in filthy condition, and have the power to stop that condition, and don, t. That show the kind of mind, you have. We have to make this world a better place to live in. Not just for the people you like. All people that need help, need to live better. There was a time in this country, where african american was living in slums ghetto. And we wanted a better life. Look at how much wealth in this country. Slums should not be on earth. At one time this country, was not sharing there wealth with african american people. What do you expect, from people you are trying to keep down?they want the same thing you want, a better live. They do what they have to do, to live better. That is why the street life, at one time look like the only way, to live better. Some time a person do things because of his condition. We need to remake the world so everbody, can have a good opportunity. Times was so hard for african american, at one time we had to do illegal things to live better. We don, t have to do illegal things, to live better today. We must work hard, and it will happen. And show more love for each other. Envy and jealousy is not helping nobody. To show love is like a brother, a brother is a helper and a protector. That is the kind of love, we need in our ethnic community. Jf we don, t we will not have unity. Back in the thirty african american were very poor. There was more unity, because we had no money. When a nigger star living better, he thinks he is better. Unity must never leave reguardless, of how much money you make. Jf the unity leave, the money have change you. What good did it do us, or you. What incentive do we have to see you get rich, and not help us. We would look forward to see you get rich, if you give back. That, s the incentive we need to see. Don, t look at wealth in a small way, look at wealth as helping people. When you used wealth in helping people, g-d will bless you. You have to understand that wealth is for to serve man with. When you understand that you should not have, a problem giving. Something is wrong with your thinking, if you think your wealth is just for yourself. How can anyone just want to use there wealth for themselves, with all this hunger in the world. Some people are so poor they cannot aford, to buy shoes. Things that are a necessity, everbody should have. Would you like to be hunger, and bear foot?we have to stop poverty!we have enough money, in the world to stop poverty. Jn fact there is more then enough to go around. There is so much greed in the world, the more you get the more you want. Look at the people who are suffering because of your greed. Jf you were not so greedy, you would be giving more, charity is a must. New york city have a lots of homeless people, and i know the city have the money to give them affordable housing. When they can go out, and buy a new yankee stadium, that the city did not need. Homeless people do not have nowhere to live, the yankee had somewhere to play baseball. You should not have to work no more, then one job to pay your rent. Some homeless people just don, t make enough money to pay this hight rent. We have the resources to house everbody. Reguardless of how much money, somebody make. Think about the small children that need your help, that are crying out for help. Jf somebody don, t go to them, they will stay in that condition. And we should not let the children, suffer. All children should be rise in a decent invironment. J tell my children it is better to give then to receive. You may think it is better to receive, because somebody is giving you something. We should not want to be in a position, where somebody have to give you something. It is better to give then receive. Some country are so poor you have know choice, but to beg. Some things in life you should know to do, without someone telling you. And when you give you don, t see color, you see a humenbeing. Jf you see color you may not give, to everbody in need. Jf you see a person as a humanbeing you will give, that is how you are suppose to see people. Jf you were down and out, you would want help. Jf everbody do there part, we can change the world by giving. Do your fair share of giving. And we should be fast in giving, not slow. Jf a person is hunger, you don, t want to wait too long to eat. Jf you wait too long, you are going to do what you have to do, and that may be illegal. A person with a good heart, is always going to give. Because he understand what wealth is for. And you can give your time to a good cause. J was standing up in the train, there was a elder person walking in, know one got up to let her set down. Giving your seat to someone, who need to sat down is chirity. And soon as you get in trouble, you call on g-d. Jf you are always giving, you have nothings to worry about, when you are in trouble. The person that need chirity, is in trouble too. That, s why he need help. No body should be overlook. Look how josephine baker was giving in her life. She did not see color, at one time she was the richest african american, women in the world. Starting on the american vaudevill circuit, success takes josephine to paris where her semi-nude dancing causes an internationl sensation. Josephine adopted twelve children, of all races a rainbow. Josephine said there is one thing that you will never, get punish for is giving!giving is the only way we can stop poverty, and together we can do it. You should not feel good about yourslef, with all this poverty in the world, and you know you can help. Why do some people make too much money, and so many don't make enough. Jf people make a livable wage, they would not have to depend on government subsidy. As long as you have people, making too much money you are going to have poverty. You have to spread wealth around, for everbody. Sometimes people will do something because of there condition. Jf you can't pay your rent, what will you do?i believe you should be patient, and keep doing the right things. You can have too much weath, and that is the way this world is. It's easy to wait if you already, have money. It's hard to wait and be patient, with no money in your pocket. Some people will try to take, something that is not there. That's why so manny african american are in prison. Jceberg slim said he try to get, something for nothing, and when you try to get something, for nothing one way or other, you are going to lose. That is one of the reason whyafrican american, are in prison some want something for nothing. And we don't have favorable opportunity. We cannot let that stop us. It's better to work and earn a honest living. That way you want go to prison, and you will feel go about yourself. What person with any sense would feel good being lock up. You have to change the way you are living, and that would make a big difference. Give yourself back to your ethnic community, and stay out. Rasool was in prison, and he would teach inmate how to stay out of prison. There was a honorary dinner for him, i was there. There were exinmate there, they were talking about how rasool help them to stay out. Staying out of prison, is giving back to your ethnic community in a big way. J don, t think it's smart to keep going, in and out of prison. There have to be something that is not right with you, you need to pray, paryer change things. Something have to happen that will stop you, from going. Some people are just lazy, and don't want to work. J have been hearing this all my life, if you don't work you are going to steal!or look for some easy way to make money. And the right way is always the hard way. And the wrong way is always the easy way. IT is better to choose the right way, that way you want have to worry, about going to prison. Staying out of prison is a way of giving back. You can't help yourself or nobody lockup. Jf you don't work how are you going to earn money?if you just refuse to work, we have to put you some where. A theft don't care who he steal from. We don't want a theft in our community. We are not in the early thirty, when we african american were very poor. That street mentaiity that we had then, have to change. We can make it without being street hustler. We need to stop thinking, and talking like that. We don't want our children growing up with a street mentaiity. Stop raping about the street life, like it is a good life to live. Some kids are inpress by the street life, that's what they want. We want our children to be inpress by people who earn a honest living. We need to keep that kind of life, in front of them. The neighbrohood you life in, don't have to be a bad neighbrohood. It can be a good place for everone to live in. And when you say bad neighbrohood, you don't want to just think of people of color, we all have false. We have to make 0ur neighbrhood safe, and clean. We all want to feel safe in our neighbrhood. J was rideing on a crowd bus in newyork, and there was a disable person got on. One person said one of those, kids should get up. The father got bad, and said don't talk to my kids that way. One of them should have got up. When i was a boy my parent would have said to me get up, and let her say down. And you want to live, a prosperous life. And you want give your seat up to a older person, we have to teach our children, to respect our elder. A lots of the children, are out of control. Children that are more respectfull, have more respect for the law. All children should frist respect, there parent. My son used to disrespect me, i would tell him what he is doing is not right. Why would you hurt the hand, that feed you. Your parent is why you are here. One day it got so bad, i call the police not to protect me, to protect him, i did not want to hurt my son. J have herd some people say, if one of my kids disrespect me i will kill'em. You will feel very bad if you did that, because you love your kids. The singer marvin gaye father kill him, and he feel very bad, because he regret what he did. Some things in life you don't want, to regret. J would have regret hurting my son. Jf you don't have a choice, that's differren. It's always better to walk away. You don't want to be the aggresor. That's why we have violence in the world. Giving will do more good, then a aggress behavior. J was watching judge karen mills on tv. There was a person on her show, suing a dog grooming company for threehundred and fifty dollar. And she said some people just don't know, what to do with there money. She said she see no reason, to have a cat groom. You could take that money to a homeless shelter.

There are a lots of people in the world, that spend money like that. When they could be giving back, look around you. And you will see people suffering all around, in the world. And you will see rich people, all around you. Rich people can aford to have there salary cut, so other can make more money, they already make too much money. When some make too much, it hurts people that don't make enough. It have to be a reason why people are in poverty. J believe the reason is greed, greed do not help people live better. Giving is what help people live better, and we all should want that. Jf a person is down, and out and you help him get on his feet, that is giving. We all want help when we are experience hard times, i know i do. Giving can stop a lots of problem in the world. Some things happen in the world because, people just don't have enough to live on. Slavery was poverty for the slaves in american, look how they were living, and how the whites were living. Slavery was the worst kind of poverty. The white man wanted to keep the slaves in poverty, they did not want the slaves to have a better life. Somethings in life man cannot stop only g-d can. Some slaves would run away to live better, and they should have. Man do not have the right to keep, no one dwon. Man do have the right to help people live better, that's what he supose to do. This world can not keep going the way it's going, poverty have to stop. It would be better for all of man kind. When you give it make you a better parson, and that mak e a better world. Jf this was a better world g-d would not allow so many problems, with the weather happen. Look how the weather destroy things, that happen for a reason. Star giving more, and you will see a change in the weather. The best way to serve g-d is to give!, g-d will protect good people. As long as you are good you have nothing to worry about, no matter how things look. It don't look good to see people suffering, when they don't have to. All politician talk shit, they never do aii they say. J am not saying there is no good politician, because there is. What the average person is fighting for, politician already have it, good pay good health care. They all stay the same shit, vote for me i will make it better. Things get much better for them, then it do for the average person. No matter who is in office you still have people suffering, politcians need to do a better job. They have the power to do so. They are using there power, to help people who don't need help, that is not good government. Good government help people, who need help the most frist. That's the kind of government we need to live under. That's why this country loved john f. Kenndy. The honarble elijah muhammad said to malcom x, this country loved this man. And we should love, someone who help the most need it ones frist. And african american loved president john f. Kenndy. At that time we was in need, the most. Jf we want more african american, to be profesional we have to stop them from going to prison. There are a lots of intelligent minds in prison. Just think if those same minds, say i am going to go straight, look at what you will have. We have to change that street mind. That's why they keep going to prison. IT come down to you, and the way you think, and the way you live your life. Can't you see that, you have no one to blame but yourself. We all need to do positive things, to stop the prison population. It would help if the raper, don't rap about the street life. We don't want to depend on that, kind of life to make a living. Some say this is all i khow, is the street. That's not true, because there is others that earn a hones living. And they came up the same way as you did. Jf that's all you see is the street life, that's what it will be. Change the way you think, and the way you live your life. By doing that you will see a big deference, in your life. You will no longer be in the prison system

S. Jceberg slim change the way he was living, and it made a diference in his life. He stop going to prison. This is a man that graduate from high school, at fifteen years old. Got a scholarship to go to college, and he got exspell. Because he was doing things that was illegal. Just think if he had stay, on the right path. Look at the good he could, have done. Like he said what attract him to be a pimp, was the glimmer. All that street life mentalati, stared when we could not do better. Now we can do better, we have to stop that way of thinking. We don't want to glimmer rise the street life. We have to keep putting back, in our ethnic community to stop it. Don't let the glimmer, of a drug dealer influence you, look at how his life end. We have to let more positive things, in our community, we need to keep feeding on that. Just keep feeding positive things back, soon that will be the glimmer. Seeing people earn a honest living, have to be the glimmer. My son let the glimmer of drug dealer, influence him. He would tell me there was, a young boy saleing drugs. And he had so much money in his pocket, it was hard to get his money out. There was one other drug dealer, he was seventeen years old, and my son said he is bad, because he carry a gun. J said he is not bad, and from now on if you don't, have something constructive too talk to me we can't converse. That kind of life look good to him. What look good is not always, the best. He had to learn that the hard way. Because he did time in prison, for drugs. When he frist stared to sale drugs, i said to him don't you know you can get a lots, of time in prison. He said to me do the crime, do the time. After that i did not said much more, he had made his decision. A friend of mind said to me that's easy to say, the older you get it's hard doing them years. When he was in jail, i went to go visit him, he ask me is it ok for him to cry. J said yes, but went you were out there doing what you were doing, you were not crying so why cry now. Sometime it's to late to cry, you need to cry befor you do the crime. Most criminal don't feel sorry into that get caught. Because things don't look good, at all for them. Jf you do the right things in life, things will look better for you. Life will always be in favor of right. We cannot blame the whiteman, if we don't make it in life, we have to take responsibility. The whiteman is not stoping you from getting a head. You don't have a good reason, to break the law. Having respect for each other, and the law can do a lots of good. You want have a reason to hurt your brother, if you do that. We have to make good of our life, wile we live, good deeds bear fruit. We all should want that. The way you live your life have a lots, to do how life end for you. One way to have a good ending is giving. There are too many people in need, to not give. Something have to be wrong, because there is still poverty. Somebody is doing something that is not right, because we still have the same problem. Look at newyork city there are to many, homeless people living there. Some problem should not be there, and homeless is one of them. Because there is too much money in this country. Giving can solve a lots of problems. Jf there were more fordable homes, that would help. A good leader help the ones who need help the most, no matter where you live in the world. Life is about what you can give. You don't want to go throw life, just receiving. It's better to give then receive. The more you give the more you will be bless. Don't just think of blessing as material things. Some people if they don't see material things, they feel they are not bless.

Blessing can come in many ways, like good health. We all want to look, and feel good. That makes a person feel good about, himself. It's hard for a person to feel good about himself, in poverty. That's like having no money in your pocket. When you get some money you feel better. There are people that don't know what it feel like to be broke. Jf you don't have no money it's hell!the best way to show someone who don't know what it feel like, take them around people in poverty. Don't just look at the rich side, look at the poor side too. Jf it bother you to see people in poverty, you will help. What more can i say about giving, or poverty without repeating myself. Jf more time is spend on giving, the world will be more at peace. That put you in the right frame, of mind. Retiring from your job, is a form of giving. That give someone else a chance to work. Some of us work too long, and you don't have to. That have to stop, let a younger person have your job, he need the job the most. Think of other people in a giving way, there are eough selfish people in the world. You can never have enough giver in the world. There will always be room for givers. There are no blessing for being selfish. You may be rich, why gain the world, and lose your soul. When you can just be a giving person. You will gain more blessing from giving. Life have prove that to be a fact. Can any one say any thing differen, then that?life work that way when you give. Life is not in your favor, when you don't give back. You may think life is in your favor, because you have money. There is a heaven and a hell. Rich people are going to be in hell, just like some poor people. It all depend on how you live your life. Some are a better person, not being rich. Money can change the way you think, not in a good way. Because you have money give into you can't, give no more. There are some that is holding back. Look at the people that are harting, that should want you to give. No one want to be in poverty, i am sure you don't. That is why people go where, they can live better. We have to give to our ethnic community frist, and then give outside. There are too many in porerty, and so few giving. When i say give, give on your income level, if you make millions give millions. Jf you make billions, give billions. You don't need all that money know way. Jf you did you would not have so much money. Some people just let money pile, up and up. That's not doing nobody, no good. What good is it to have money if you, don't used it. Money should be used in the right way. Look at all the ways, you can spend your money to help people. Sometimes that's all a person need, is some help. You have to understand, what wealth is for. How do you rate your giving, good or bad?your giving should be rated good. No one should have bad rateing, in giving. J would love to see the rate of african amercian, stop going to prison. When that happen we will have a safer community. We don't want people to feel, uncomfortable around us. When you have a lots, of criminal in your neighbrohood, what do you expect, you have to be on guard. Jf a person is down and out, he already feel bad about himself. Don't say negative things about him. You don't want to kick, someone because he is down. You want to motivate him, to feel good about himslef. When that happen he will do better. Jf someone with some money help, that can solve a lots of problem, and go a long way. There are still a lots of african american, that is doing positive things. We have to have unity to have our own community. You should not say i got my'em, we all should have it as a whole, that is how it should be. A family want to see all family member, do good. J don't want to see my brothers, and sisters suffering. J am not just talking about my race all races. The world will be more at peace, if there were not greed. Greed is not going to stop people, from suffering. Greed just keep taking, and taking. The more it gets the more it wants. The world do not need, people like that. The world need people that can make this world a better place, that's what the w0rld need. Jf you cannot make this world a better place, you need to change. The world cannot stay in the condition that it's in. Poverty cannot keep going, from one generation to the next. Somethings in the world we can stop, and some condition should not be. J think everbody should have health insurance. Just like everbody should have there, own place to live in. We are talking about basic things in life. It's hard to live without the basic things, in life. No one should have to live like that. Jf people did not make too much money, the people that don't make enough will have more. Wealth have t0 be balance, for ever one. You should not have too much on one side, that's what's worng with the world. Look at the people that have so litte, and trying to get by. That's how hard life is for some, life should be easy for everbody. And together we can make that happen. You want life to be good to you and it can, some are always giving. Jf you can aford to that's what you do. And life will be good to you. The people 0n top in all form of life, make too much money. And the people on bottom, make so litte. We all want nice homes, money in our pocket. Jf you make millions, it would not hurt you if you make less. That money can be balance out, in other people salary. J don't wanta free hand out. J want to earn enough money to buy the things i need, just like you. That is a good deed giving to people. It's better to help people earn, there living. That's why people need to earn good wages, so they want need help. What do you expect from pepole that don't earn, enough money to live out of. Help have to come from some where. Regurdless of your income level you should, live in decent, safe, and sanitary housing. Everbody is not going to make the same money. That is why we have to make sure, everbody is take in care of. Nobody should have too much wealth, when there are people suffering. That is proof wealth is not balance. The mayor of new york city makes over two hundred thousand a year. And he gets free housing, at the tax payor exspense. And you have thousand, of new yorker that are homeless. Something is worng with that. There are a lots of situations, that need to be change. Because some have too much. You will not stop poverty, leting people have too much money. The rich will just keep getting richer, and the people will stay in poverty. You have to put wealth, where it is most need it. Just keep putting wealth there, to there is no more poverty. That's how you stop poverty. You are not going to stop nothing, being a pig!some company don't give rises like they should. They want to make all the money. And pay the worker, very litter money. But want you to work hard for them. Company like that should not be in business. The less you make, the more they make. Look at what worker make for company, and what the workers get pay. Greed calls a lots of pain, and suffering. Some people sale things that are harmful, because of greed, some even kill. That's how bad some want money. A person that's a giver will not do that. G-d for bid greed!the world need to teach giving, look at how jean shafiroff is giving back. She said it is the duty of the schools to teach our children the importance of giving. We need more people like that. N0 matter how rich or poor you are, you should have favorable opertuity. We all should have equal opertuity. Greed and jealousy can stop things, from happening. Jf there were more giving, there would be pleace. And there would not be all this natural destruction in the world. G-d allow things to happen when man is not living right. Jf we all just give we all can have heaven, on earth. And this world would be so much better. Living in a world where there is peace, all around you. That's what giving can do for you. Greed will lead you to the hell fire!and no one can help, save yourself. Don't be the one to say, i wish i had give more of my wealth, right now is your time, so don't waste it. Or you will be sorry, in the long run. Because you want like the situation, you are in. G-d did not just created the world for you, to live good. He want all mankind to live good, give so everbody have a chance. Look how well people do with good opportunity. Look at the history of african american, went they were being held down, they all were poor. Because of better opportunity things got better. Some people make so much money, they can aford to take a cut in pay. That will make things better. You can have so much money, you spend because you have money. You should never forget, about the people who need help the most, that is where you give more. Giving is receiving, when you give you will get something from it, that's all i am saying is give, you cannot go wrong. You have g-d on your side!don't just look at your blessing in material things. It's a blessing to not go, on the wrong path. Money will not get you to heaven. Money will help if you used it, the right way. Useing money in

The wrong way, will send you to hell!that's like having bad luck!if you want to have good luck give. That's not to say you are not going to have problems, life can be good even with the problems. One way or other you will pay for not giving, everbody should give there fair share. And that would solve the poverty problem. And the world would be poverty free. That's how life suppose to be. J don't feel bad because, i am giving my fair share. We all should feel that way. T0 say there is not enough, is like saying g-d made a mistake. G-d is perfect!for ever baby that is born g-d have all ready provide for. What the babyneed it's already, in creation. All humanbeing should not live in, filth foul dirty condition. We have to live, like we are humanbeing. H0w can y0u say you are a good leader, when you have people living like that. You are onfit to be a leader. A good leader help the people, who need help the most, are you being help the most, because you need help the most?in my conclusion don't say, i got my own fuck you!when you don't give back that's what you are saying. When i was growing up i had a older borther, levi was not the kind of older brother, that you can say can i have a few dollars. J remember when i was about twelve years old. J ask tommy junior who is not my brother for a dime. He said go ask your brother levi. J did not want to ask him, because i know he was going to say something stupid. He yell at me sayjng don't ask me for money!i walk a way tommy junior, walk up to me and ask me did levi give you some money, i said no!he look like he could not believe he said no. He went in his pocked and gave me a dime. Charity star at home and spread. Anybody should feel comfortably about asking there older, brother for money. My sister ideborah had a boyfreind we call him pie. He was more of a, older brother then levi. Sometime he would give you money without asking. And would say something positive to you. You don't need someone tearing you down, that was how levi was. Jf you cannot say something, piositive don't say nothing. A brother is a helper and a protector, i am not just talking about blood brothers. You have to be strong to not let negative, people hold you down. Just keep onpushing!whatever you give back try for it to be long lasting. Don't just come back and give something, that will only last one day. Business schools, and apartments, last a long time. Success is when you are happy!you don't have to have a lots of money, to have success. Some people are rich, and not happy!we need to make everbody happy, by living above the poverty level. To all people that give back, may g-d bless you!

Printed in the United States
By Bookmasters